THE STORY OF THE
RED ARROWS

Colin Higgs

THE STORY OF THE
RED ARROWS

First published in the UK in 2014

© G2 Entertainment 2021

www.g2books.co.uk

Printed and bound in Europe

ISBN 978-1-78281-647-8

Contents

4 – 7   Introduction

8 – 21   The RAF on display

22 – 27   The Folland Gnat

28 – 41   Red Arrows - Year One

42 – 53   The Gnat Years

54 – 65   The Hawk

66 – 75   Red Arrows - The Hawk Years

76 – 91   Red Arrows - A Year in the Life

92 – 107   Red Arrows - Flying the Flag

108 – 121   The Red Arrows have competition!

122 – 125   Past, Present and Future

Introduction

BELOW Folland Gnat XS101 of the 1978 Red Arrows prepares to take off for another spectacular display

The Red Arrows, officially the Royal Air Force Aerobatic Team, is the world's greatest display team. That's a bold statement but everywhere they go their precision displays and skilful flying in their distinctive bright red Hawks draws enormous crowds. They top the billing all over the world promoting British industry, representing the Royal Air Force and giving great entertainment.

ABOVE A Red Arrows classic bomb burst

The public face is nine pilots flying their aircraft but behind the scenes there is an organisation of more than 100 people. The pilots wear red flying suits and the ground crew wear blue. There is Red 10 who co-ordinates the season, flies the spare aircraft and commentates at air shows. The 'Blues' are fitters,

ABOVE The show can't go on without them! The Red Arrows ground crew, 'The Blues', take a few moments out from their work while the Red Arrows fly their display at Farnborough in 2006

engineers, airframe specialists, drivers, photographers, people who look after the g-suits and survival equipment and a team responsible for the dye that produces the smoke trails that add so much to the displays. There is the 'circus', nine engineers who fly in the back seats of the Hawks to every display to look after the aircraft while away from base. There is flight operations, planning, administration and public relations.

A team like this has kept the Red Arrows in the forefront of British aviation for almost 60 years. The pilots live and breathe flying, working in an intense atmosphere where their first mistake could be their last. The support team keep the aircraft flying with the knowledge that OK isn't good enough. Every aircraft has to be in perfect shape for every display.

The result is spectacular and hopefully the Red Arrows will go on for many more years.

Colin Higgs

ABOVE: LEFT The team manoeuvre in formation with their undercarriage down RIGHT The Diamond Bend at Finningley in 1983

BELOW: LEFT The Red Arrows at Mildenhall in 1989 RIGHT The end of another great display with the Vixen Break

Chapter 1

The RAF on display

BELOW The Avro Flying School. This was how pilots learned to fly in the post First World War years

THE FIRST DISPLAYS

The Diamond Nine is probably the most famous manoeuvre of the Red Arrows' display. It's a move that has thrilled crowds all over the world for almost 60 years. But these displays are more than just entertainment. They present a dazzling shop window for British industry, coaxing export orders from countries around the world.

They inspire the men and women

LEFT Gloster Meteor T7s of the CFS Meteorites display team in 1953. The first RAF team to be given a name

THE RAF ON DISPLAY

IMAGE Formation of four 5FTS de Havilland Vampire T.11s replaced by the Gnat in 1962

who serve in the Royal Air Force and command the respect and support of the public, the taxpayers who ultimately pay the bill.

For almost 100 years such performances have helped the RAF keep its independence because during its entire existence it has been under attack from forces at the very heart of power in Britain.

When the guns fell silent on 11 November 1918 at the end of the First World War the RAF had only been in existence for eight months but was the largest air force in the world. They had bombers that could fly 1,000 miles, reaching Berlin and back, having dropped 2,500lbs of bombs but the end of the war meant that the RAF had never had the chance to show its potential. The "war to end all wars" had been costly and over the next few years the Royal Air Force found itself undermined by lack of investment. Politicians believed that the RAF had only been created to help win the war and that the end of the conflict should signal the end of the service.

RAF commanders expected some reduction but within two years the strength had been cut from 399 squadrons to just 41 and personnel was cut by 90%. The demise of the RAF seemed certain. However the increasing popularity of air displays allowed the RAF to demonstrate what the war had not been able to, that taxpayers money was being well spent.

Flying aircraft covered in bright silver dope the display pilots dazzled the crowds which gathered to watch.

In the face of government antipathy, RAF supremo Air Marshal Sir Hugh Trenchard quickly realised the value of this publicity and encouraged his peacetime squadrons to form their own display teams. Each year a different squadron was nominated as the official RAF team.

The first Hendon air display took place in 1920 in front of more than 60,000 people. They came to watch formation flying and aerobatic feats using the aircraft that had helped win the war. The Hendon air show quickly

BELOW The Redskins display team from CFS in 1958. Two Jet Provost T.1s

ABOVE Line up of Jet Provost T.3s of CFS at Little Rissington in 1959

became established as part of the summer social season and there were many in the crowds who had influence.

For the RAF formation flying was a great way to perfect pilot skills as it meant that the pilots had to practice regularly. Many of the manoeuvres were based on actual combat techniques developed during the Great War. Thus it was believed that the ability to fly in unison and harmony would pay immense dividends should the pilots ever have to go to war again.

RECORD BREAKING

Air racing and record breaking also caught the imagination of the public during the 1920s and 30s and provided reasons to the aircraft manufacturers to put money into development of new

aircraft despite a lack of orders from the RAF in times of military budget cuts. In June 1919 two former RAF aircrew, John Alcock and Arthur Whitton Brown flew a Vickers Vimy across the Atlantic non-stop, a feat unimaginable just a few years earlier. Future Spitfire test pilot Alex Henshaw set a new speed and time record flying from London to Cape Town and back. As he said in an interview "to be the best, or the fastest, or the highest, has always been the goal of pilots and manufacturers alike. As soon as a record was set it had to be beaten. The pilots became the superstars of their day."

Three Vickers Wellesleys, flown by RAF pilots, set the long distance record in 1938 by flying non-stop from Cairo to Australia; over 7,000 miles in 48 hours! These were the first aircraft to be built with a new strong and durable lattice framework designed by Barnes Wallis, the man who later designed the Wellington bomber and the bouncing bomb used by the Dambusters.

Possibly the greatest publicity for the RAF was the Schneider Trophy. Air racing had become big box-office and international competitions offered impressive prizes and the possibility of commercial success. The most coveted award was the Schneider Trophy fought over 13 times between 1913 and 1931. The organisers wanted it to encourage technical advances in seaplane design but it ended up as a pure speed race.

BELOW The six Jet provosts of The Red Pelicans taking off in formation at the SBAC Show at Farnborough in September 1964

THE RAF ON DISPLAY

IMAGE The five Jet Provost T.4s of The Red Pelicans in 1963

The rules said that three victories in succession won the trophy outright. British teams flying British designed and built aircraft and flown by RAF aircrew won it in 1927 in Venice and again in 1929 in England at Calshot on the south coast. More than 200,000 people made the trek back to Calshot in 1931 to see whether Britain could win the trophy outright. David Green, a future Spitire pilot, was inspired to fly by his visit to the trophy races "we went up to Gosport in our open tourer and it was a totally different world in those days. We camped out on South beach near the pier and there were thousands of people there who had come from all over England to see the event. There was a tremendous air of festivity, Punch and Judy shows, and ice cream men, it was a real gala day. I remember there was a Royal Navy destroyer moored off the beach and it had a tall black and white pylon on it which was one of the turning points. Before long this incredible aircraft snarled round this pylon opposite us. I shall never forget that day." The RAF crew won the day and the trophy outright.

The winning aircraft, the Supermarine S6B was designed by RJ

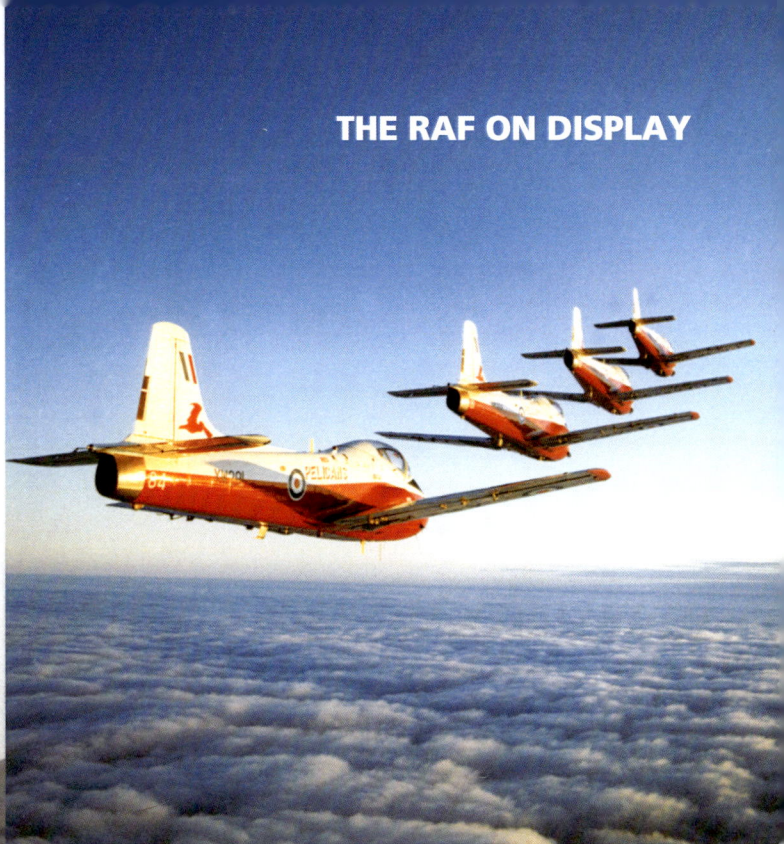

Mitchell. The success of the aircraft inspired him to design perhaps the greatest aircraft of the Second World War, the Supermarine Spitfire.

These long-distance flights, record breaking feats and thrilling air displays did more than raise the profile of the RAF. They also forced military strategists to think long and hard about the use of air power in future conflicts. In many ways they helped to persuade politicians to consider the future of the RAF as a separate service and to begin to unlock the national purse and spend money on developing the aircraft that would eventually help to win the war. They also persuaded many thousands of young men and women that a career in the RAF and the chance to fly was an exciting opportunity.

The Second World War was obviously not a time for the RAF to put on air displays. But millions of Britons watched nightly as formations of Lancasters and Halifaxes flew off to attack enemy territory and every morning a few less returning. The Battle of Britain was fought over the heads of Londoners and people living in the south east of England and in 1944 great

ABOVE LEFT The Macaws, the four Jet Provost T.4s from the College of Air Warfare in 1968

ABOVE RIGHT The Red Pelicans in the last colour scheme in 1973

ABOVE Jet Provost T.4 of 1FTS in the last year of the Linton Gin display team, 1969

FAR RIGHT The five black Hunters from 111 Squadron's 1957 Black Arrows' climb vertically

armadas of transport aircraft and gliders set out to deliver paratroopers to the Normandy countryside, Arnhem and across the Rhine. Britain was left in no doubt that the RAF was playing its part.

THE JET AGE

The end of the war saw not only the expected reduction from a wartime air force to peacetime but the need again to promote the RAF and keep them in the public eye. The annual anniversary of the battle of Britain saw the beginning of the RAF At Home Days, when RAF air stations opened their doors and let the public in. But now it was the late 1940s and there was a new sound in the sky as the air shows ushered in a new era of jets.

FARNBOROUGH

The Society of British Aircraft Companies started a new show initially at Radlett in Hertfordshire and eventually at Farnborough in Hampshire where it has stayed ever since. Farnborough had been the site of aircraft development and testing since before the First World War and was a superb location to show off the best of British aviation. Rapidly the Farnborough Air Show became the place for British manufacturers to display and meet potential customers from round the world. Each show culminated in a spectacular air display. It was an annual show then and the flying displays were packed with new aircraft. The Bristol Brabazon and the prototype of the Comet, the first jet airliner, flew for the first time in public in 1949. 1955 saw Avro test pilot, Roly Falk, slow roll the Vulcan, not something that was allowed at an air show again! The Short SC-1 became the first aircraft to take off vertically at the 1959 show before the Harrier forerunner, the P.1127, was displayed in 1962.

As the British aircraft industry contracted in the 1960s the SBAC had to allow overseas aircraft for the first time. Initially, in 1966, foreign aircraft were allowed as long as they had British engines but by 1974 they had to let in all overseas aircraft manufacturers. Now the biggest chalets and static displays come from the American giants such as Boeing and Lockheed. However one great element of the air show that has never changed is the RAF displays.

The 1950s and 60s were the heyday of the RAF squadron display teams. 54, 64 and 600 Squadrons all flew Meteor teams while 72 Squadron flew Vampires. When the Hawker Hunter came into service 111 Squadron's team changed from flying four Meteors to four gloss black painted Hunters, then to seven and eventually nine under the command of Squadron Leader Roger Topp. The team gained a name, the

Black Arrows, and received proper recognition as the RAF official display team in 1956.

Topp trained to fly during the war but a surplus of pilots meant he became a glider pilot, taking part in the crossing of the River Rhine in 1945. After the war he resumed flying powered aircraft and joined 98 Squadron on Mosquitoes. In 1950 he passed his test pilot's course at the Experimental Test Pilots School (ETPS) before resuming his RAF flying career. He became CO of 111 Squadron in 1955 and successfully led both the squadron and the display team for three years.

At the Farnborough Air Show of 1958 Topp got permission from the RAF to try to beat the world looping record which stood at sixteen aircraft. He 'borrowed' pilots from other squadrons, increased the numbers and astonished the crowd on each day of the air show by starting the squadron display with a 22 ship loop, a record that has never been beaten. In 1961 92 Squadron, one of the most famous Battle of Britain Spitfire squadrons, took over the mantle of official team and flew a team of Hunters called The Blue Diamonds.

By this time many of the front line squadrons were re-equipping with the latest, and first British supersonic, jet fighter, the English Electric Lightning.

ABOVE Crawford Cameron of 92 Squadron's Blue Diamonds glances at the photographers before take off at Farnborough in 1962

FAR LEFT The ultimate air show display? The twenty-two Hunters of 111 Squadron's Black Arrows loop at the SBAC Show at Farnborough in 1958

THE RAF ON DISPLAY

ABOVE LEFT Sixteen Hawker Hunters of 92 Squadron's Blue Diamonds

ABOVE RIGHT Two images of 74 Squadron's Tigers display team in the early years of the supersonic Lightning

In 1960 74 Squadron had become the first to receive the brand new Lightning, a handful for experienced pilots used to flying subsonic aircraft. At the same time they were expected to put out a nine ship display team while getting to know their aircraft for the first time. The Tigers, as they were known, barely had nine aircraft serviceable for train-ing let alone for full public displays but they managed two searing displays at Farnborough and Paris that year. Commanding Officer Squadron Leader John Howe found himself torn between learning to operate this new powerful beast and creating beautiful displays for the public. It was sheer professionalism that kept the squadron flying and displaying. The Tigers flew for three years before handing over to 56 Squadron, the Firebirds.

By 1964 the RAF were concerned about the amount of time individual front line squadrons were spending on working up aerobatic routines rather than on combat training.

The Flying Schools had their own teams of course, rejoicing in names such as The Meteorites, The Macaws,

The Redskins and even the 'Gin-Four' Flying instructors used formation aerobatics as part of their everyday training and therefore there was good reason to operate these teams and let the front line squadrons get on with their primary role.

Although many of the squadrons retained their display teams for a while the responsibility for the official RAF team moved to the training squadrons based at the Flying Training Schools.

BELOW LEFT Lightning F Mk1 74 Squadron "Tigers"

BELOW RIGHT Hunting Percival Jet Provost T.4s of The Red Pelicans 1964

Chapter 2

The Folland Gnat

THE FOUNDING OF AN AVIATION BUSINESS

Folland is not the best known name in British aviation but the man who started the company, Henry Folland, deserves a place in a list of great British aircraft designers. Born in 1889 he worked in the automobile business for Lanchester and Daimler before his interest in flying led him to change trades and join the Royal Aircraft Factory at Farnborough. Here he led a led a team that designed the SE4, SE5 and SE5A, one of the best British fighters of the First World War. He moved to Nieuport in 1917 where he was responsible for the Goshawk and Nighthawk fighters. The Nighthawk was a radial engined biplane which set a trend for RAF fighters which Folland would continue when he joined Gloster Aircraft in 1921.

During the 1920s and 30s Gloster provided the RAF with many aircraft in their post-war rebuilding period. The Gloster Grebe, which entered service in 1924, became famous as the aircraft that excited the crowds at the 1925 Hendon Air Display when 25 Squadron performed close formation flying and thrilling aerobatics. The Grebe was rapidly followed by the Gamecock and eventually the Gauntlet, the RAF's final open-cockpit fighter biplane. The last and most modern of Folland's inter-war designs for the RAF was the Gladiator, the final biplane fighter to enter service with the RAF.

Folland's final design for Gloster was a monoplane fighter built in response to the RAF's requirement for a specific

K7810

K 781

ABOVE Gloster Gauntlet designed by Henry Folland and flown by the RAF from 1935

aircraft that would operate in the Far East. Two prototypes were built and test pilots loved the aircraft but the Spitfire and Hurricane had both been ordered so the specification was cancelled.

In 1937 Henry Folland became managing director of an aircraft business on the River Hamble in Hampshire. British Marine had been set up to build Sikorsky flying boats under license but the company had failed and the refinanced company became Folland Aircraft Ltd. Throughout the Second World War the company took on the subcontracted building of other aircraft. Fuselages for 15,000 Spitfires were built in the factory, part of the great dispersal of aircraft building in Britain when major aircraft factories were threatened by German bombing raids. The company also built parts for Beauforts, Wellingtons and Mosquitoes while Henry Folland attempted to get support for his own designs.

At the end of the war the company struggled to find work. Geared up for the frenzy of wartime production the orders dropped off and they turned their hand to building anything that people would buy. Fridges and bedroom furniture were just two of the items they built before the aviation work continued, still subcontracted work mainly from de Havilland and Bristol.

The Folland Gnat makes its first appearance at Farnborough in 1959

FAR RIGHT The prototype Gnat goes vertical for the cameras

THE MAN FROM ENGLISH ELECTRIC

Another aircraft designer who deserves more recognition is WEW "Teddy" Petter, the man responsible for the Lysander while he worked at Westland and the classic Canberra and P.1, forerunner of the Lightning, at English Electric.

Petter was concerned about the increasing cost, size and weight of fighters and wanted to pursue designs for lighter and more cost effective aircraft rather than the heavyweight Lightning. Realising there was no future for him at English Electric he resigned and became deputy Managing Director of Folland Aircraft in 1950 replacing Henry Folland as managing director the following year. Folland himself was ill and somewhat disillusioned with the lack of interest in his own designs but there could be nobody better to take on the role than Petter.

Petter's first lightweight design was for a single seat fighter called the Midge. The Midge flew for the first time in August 1954, the same month that Henry Folland died. The next version of the aircraft, now re-engined and renamed the Gnat, flew the following year. It received no RAF orders as they chose the Hawker Hunter to fulfill the proposed Gnat role. However the aircraft did get orders from Finland and India. Finland bought just 13 of the aircraft but India eventually chose it as one of their main frontline fighters. 25 Gnats were ordered direct from the Hamble factory but the Indian-based Hindustan Aeronautics built more than

200 under licence as well as an updated version called the Ajeet. The Indian Air Force operated the Gnat successfully in two wars with Pakistan.

GNATS FOR THE RAF

Despite the lack of interest for the single seat Gnat from the RAF Petter continued development of a two-seat version. The increasing complexity of RAF frontline aircraft meant that more specialist advanced trainers were needed. In the late 1950s the route to fast jet flying for a cadet was from the Jet Provost to the Vampire T.11 and onto an Operational Conversion Unit. However the difference in speed and performance between the Vampire and aircraft like the Hunter meant that trainees had to relearn flying techniques let alone methods of air warfare. With the Lightning due in service in 1960 this differential would be even greater. A faster trainer would be needed and the Gnat suited the purpose. The other vital factor was the Gnat's low cost to build and maintain, something that actually reduced the cost of RAF jet training.

14 pre-production aircraft were

THE FOLLAND GNAT

THE FOLLAND GNAT

virtually all the equipment that was used by the frontline aircraft of the time including the supersonic brand new Lightning. This meant a complete redesign of the cockpit and all its instrumentation.

The six trials Gnats that arrived at the Central Flying School at Little Rissington could fly at 40,000 feet and could go supersonic in a dive. At the same time they could fly well at the low speeds suitable for a novice jet pilot. Instructors loved the Gnat as it was sensitive to fly but provided a much better performance than the Jet Provost. It also gave them an aircraft that would really pose their students a challenge and prepare them for flying those fast frontline jets.

It was no surprise perhaps when these recently arrived trainers were chosen to form a new display team for the 1964 season. The Yellowjacks were soon followed by the Red Arrows which flew the type for a further 15 years.

Although some more Gnats were

ordered in 1958 and the first flight of the two-seat Gnat took place on 31 August 1959 and although the RAF were concerned whether a company the size of Folland could build the required number of aircraft, their merger into Hawker Siddeley later that year produced further orders.

The Gnat T.Mk.1 that entered service with the RAF in early 1962 differed from the original single seater in just a few ways. Slightly bigger wings that could hold larger fuel tanks and a longer fuselage to accommodate the two seats were the main changes but internally the changes were radical. The production contract required the cockpit to contain

ABOVE Gnat XS101 of the Red Arrows at Finningley in 1979

delivered to CFS the majority went to Valley to equip 4FTS and replace the Vampire T.11s. Although it fulfilled all the RAF's requirements there were still a few issues, most of which related to the size of the aircraft. Tall pilots, for example, simply couldn't fit and if they did, and had to eject, they were liable to suffer knee and leg injuries. Whilst easy to maintain ground crew did find they could be fiddly with so much equipment packed into a small space.

The Gnat stayed in service until phased out from 1978 and finally replaced completely by the Hawk. 4FTS graduated its final course of students in November 1979 and the Gnat was officially gone.

Perhaps surprisingly, considering how hard these aircraft were flown in RAF service, there are still plenty of Gnats flying around the world. At least 15 of the 200 built still fly and many more grace museums and airfields around the world. One sits proudly at RAF Scampton in Lincolnshire, the current home of the Red Arrows while another flies in the colours of the original Yellowjacks team. It seems that there will be Gnats around for many years to come.

Chapter 3

Red Arrows - Year One

FAR RIGHT The four Jet Provosts of The Red Pelicans

CFS AND THE RED PELICANS

Among the many RAF training establishments the Central Flying School, based at Little Rissington in Gloucestershire, had its own display team flying Jet Provosts. The Red Pelicans were the latest of a number of 'JP' teams at CFS but were their first to be equipped specially for the displays. The aircraft were bright red and carried purpose-built smoke canisters to show off their manoeuvres and formations to the public. The Red Pelicans were in great demand at air shows and displays around the country so at the end of the 1963 season it was decided they would continue as an official RAF team and replace the current squadron display team, the Firebirds of 56 Squadron, leaving them to fly their front line Lightning supersonic jet fighters in their designated role.

THE FIRST GNAT TEAM - THE YELLOWJACKS

Liverpool-born Flight Lieutenant Lee Jones was a pilot with considerable experience of display flying. He had flown Mosquito night fighters with 141 Squadron, then Meteors, Sabres and Hunters before taking his first display steps with 229 Operational Conversion Unit at Chivenor, leading their aerobatic teams on Hunters. In 1960 he joined 111 Squadron and flew in the famous Black Arrows Hunter team. Two years later Jones was posted to CFS

creation of a display team.

Jones himself credits the creation of a Gnat display team to Air Marshal Sir Richard 'Batchy' Atcherley, a famous pre-war RAF pilot who had retired and become a director of Folland Aircraft. He was anxious for a new RAF display team to use the RAF's future advanced trainer, the Gnat. When Jones was posted to CFS he lobbied many senior officers including Battle of Britain fighter ace, Air Commodore Harold Bird-Wilson who was his commandant at CFS. Official permission finally came from the AOC-in-C of Flying Training Command, Sir Augustus Walker, himself a Bomber Command veteran from the Second World War. In 1964 Lee Jones was chosen to lead the first Gnat team, the Yellowjacks.

The future of the Yellowjacks was not assured. The pilots primary role was introducing student pilots to the aircraft and instructing them in the ways of jet flight. Teething problems with the new aircraft led to a backlog of students awaiting their courses and in the first few months of the team they managed precious few display training hours. They flew various aircraft and it was June 1964 before their distinctive

ABOVE The five Gnats of the Yellowjacks and six Jet Provosts of The Red Pelicans at Farnborough in 1964

at Little Rissington to convert to the Gnat and take his instructor's course. On completion he became an instructor at Valley as a Flight Lieutenant. Teamed with the arrival of the Gnat, the first training aircraft that really flew like a fighter, it was no surprise that Jones became the driving force behind the daffodil yellow painted Gnats began to arrive. Although they were a team of five they were allocated nine aircraft with the final one arriving from the paint shop at Dunsfold in August.

The team was already popular before its first public display. When they were on training flights the local traffic on Anglesey would stop and eventually a special lay-by was built for people to park and watch the practices. A local journalist heard about these flights and asked whether he could come to the control tower to watch. Asking what they were called he heard Lee Jones' voice on the RT in the tower saying 'Yellowjack running in" and printed in his paper that the team was called the Yellowjacks. In reality the call sign was used by Jones because while on the Black Arrows the call sign was blackjack and as the aircraft were painted yellow he changed the call sign accordingly.

The first public display for the Yellowjacks was at Culdrose in Cornwall on 25 July 1964. Flight, probably the most important aviation magazine in the world, was impressed by the team's performance. Writing that "they entertained a crowd of 12,500 with their ten minute show." the article went on to say "the team performs its entire display in only a small piece of sky and is thus constantly in front of its audience."

This was music to the ears of Lee Jones, the aerobatic perfectionist.

At the Farnborough Air Show in September 1964 the season culminated in an hour long RAF display of which

BELOW The short-lived but hugely influential Yellowjacks team of Gnats from 4FTS at Valley in 1964

ABOVE A Gnat in the colours of one of the Yellowjacks display team

BELOW The Yellowjacks from 4FTS prepare for take off at Farnborough in 1964

the Yellowjacks and Red Pelicans were a major part. The Red Pelicans had flown throughout 1964 and for the latter half of the season they were often joined in co-ordinated displays by the 4FTS Gnat team flying their bright yellow Gnat trainers. So the public were treated to a six-ship team of bright red JPs together with five bright yellow Gnats. This was a revelation compared to all the black and silver that had gone before.

The Yellowjacks performed at two further shows in September and two weeks later were disbanded, the pilots returning to their day jobs after just a few weeks together in the team.

The Red Pelicans were to continue as the CFS display team until 1973 albeit as a trimmed four-ship team rather than six. The Gnats of 4 FTS, however, had caught the eye of the RAF hierarchy. It was decided to form the first official Royal Air Force display team that would be run virtually as a separate squadron, removing it from any other organisation's control but under the watchful eye of RAF Flying Training Command.

FORMING THE REDS

Early in 1965 plans for the new team began to take shape. Many types of aircraft were considered but availability, age, cost and practicality meant that the fast, swept-wing, little Gnat was chosen again despite a shortage for the flying training schools. Having succcessfully led the Yellowjacks the previous year Lee Jones was chosen to be the leader. He put together a team for 1965 chosen from the RAF's experienced instructors. It was eight pilots, the team of seven with a reserve.

No.2 and deputy to Lee Jones was Bryan Nice. Previously a merchant seaman with Shell he had joined the RAF in 1953 and flown Meteors for two years before being posted to Germany on ground-attack Venoms. In 1959 he took an instructor's course at CFS and taught on Jet Provosts. Back at CFS in 1962 he became one of the JP pilots on the Red Pelicans before being chosen for the Red Arrows.

Probably the most famous member of the team that year was Ray Hanna. Ray was a New Zealander who flew Meteors, Venoms and Hunters before becoming a flight commander at the Ferry Squadron at RAF Benson where he delivered Sabres, Hunters and Javelins. Qualifying as a flying instructor in 1962 he became a member of the College of Warfare's Meteor display team before a posting to CFS as a Gnat instructor. He became No.3 in the 1965 Red Arrows. Ray went on to become the longest

BELOW A rare picture of five Gnats from the Red Arrows at their first public display in Britain at Biggin Hill in 1965

serving Red Arrows pilot as he led the team from 1966 to 1969. Ray's fame, however, goes well past his time in the RAF. Leaving in 1971 he became a civil airline pilot for ten years before starting The Old Flying Machine Company based at Duxford airfield in 1981 with his children, Mark and Sarah. They restored classic warbirds and provided aircraft for many famous feature films including some breathtaking low flying sequences for Empire of the Sun.

One of the most spectacular sights of the air show season for many years was Ray Hanna flying Spitfire Mk. IX MH434. This Spitfire was bought in 1968 by Sir Adrian Swire, a major shareholder in Cathay Pacific Airlines, after it had been used in the filming of the film Battle of Britain. Sir Adrian contacted Ray Hanna about displaying the aircraft even before he had left the RAF. Eventually Ray went to fly for Cathay Pacific and flew their Tristars during the week and the Spitfire at the weekend. Ray's partnership with the Spitfire lasted for more than 25 years. Sadly Ray's son Mark, himself a very skilled ex-RAF Phantom pilot, was killed in an air crash in Spain in 1999. Ray himself died in 2005.

Gerry Ranscombe was No.4 for 1965. Another Liverpool man, he flew Meteor night fighters before converting to Canberras in 1959. He became an instructor at 5FTS in Oakington in 1962 before being posted to Valley. At Valley he joined Lee Jones as one of the Yellowjacks Gnat display team before being chosen for the Red Arrows.

Flying Officer Peter Hay was No.5, a Southern Rhodesian who joined the RAF as late as 1959. He flew Vampires and then Hunters in 43 Squadron before becoming an instructor. Almost immediately following his posting to Valley in January 1964 he became a member of the Yellowjacks team.

Thirty three year old Bill Loverseed was No. 6. Bill's father had been an adventurous pilot and politician, flying in the Spanish Civil War and during the battle of Britain as an RAF fighter pilot. Bill himself joined the RAF in 1950 and flew Meteors with 43 Squadron based at Leuchars in Scotland. His second tour was with 14 Squadron at Oldenburg in Germany flying Hunters before taking his instructing course at CFS. He was a member of the Meteor display team at the RAF Flying College at Manby before being posted to CFS again this

ABOVE A Red Arrows Gnat from the synchro pair

time on Gnats. Bill left the RAF in 1972 but continued flying. He was eventually killed aged 66 when his Dash 7 aircraft crashed into a hillside in Devon in 1998.

The final member, and No.7 was Flight Lieutenant Henry Prince, who was also the youngest at thirty one. He joined the RAF in 1953 and served with 56 Squadron on Meteors. Following his CFS course he instructed on Jet Provosts at 2FTS at Syerston before moving to 4FTS in 1962 and converting to Gnats. He had been the reserve pilot for the Yellowjacks in 1964.

The Red Arrows' reserve pilot in 1965 was Eric Tilsley who as a trainee in 1945 flew with the Fleet Air Arm. His planned career was a Colonial police-man in East Africa but he joined the Royal Auxiliary Air Force before re-enlisting in the RAF. He flew tactical strike Canberras from Germany with 59

THE STORY OF THE **RED ARROWS**

LEFT A Gnat with an Armstrong Whitworth Argosy used to transport the Red Arrows ground crew and all their equipment

Squadron then qualified as an instructor, initially on Chipmunks before a posting to CFS on Jet Provosts. In 1964 he was a member of the Red Pelicans display team.

These short biographies show that there was a tried and tested route for these men to become display pilots. Display flying in close formation was one of the disciplines RAF pilots had to learn and instructors were some the best formation flyers of all.

THE TEAM GET THEIR AIRCRAFT

Lee Jones wanted to lead a team of nine aircraft and pilots as that gave them the most opportunities to create formations in the display. Financial restraints, however, meant that they could only fly seven in that first year. The team was allocated ten Folland Gnats, five of which had been flown by the Yellowjacks the previous year and repainted in Post Office red. They were delivered from the Dunsfold paint shop during the late winter and spring so the team had its full complement by the beginning of the display season. They carried the CFS crest, the RAF roundels and various white flashes. The aircraft were standard T.Mk.1 Gnats but had better radios and smoke canisters added. By injecting a mix of diesel and coloured industrial dye into the jetstream of the aircraft the Gnats could pour red, white or blue smoke. The team's equipment and ground crew were carried by an RAF twin-boom Armstrong Whitworth Argosy transport aircraft.

The ground crew were all part of the display team as well. Whether practicing at their home base or on show to the public the engineers were drilled by line chief Jock Hutson. He demanded that the aircraft and engineers looked their best on the ground. With the aircraft in a straight line and the engineers dressed in immaculate white overalls the team was ready for their introduction to the public.

THE TEAM GETS A NAME

The name of the team came from two sources. The Red Pelicans had been the official RAF team so it was decided to keep using Red in the name. The Gnats were painted mainly red anyway so it made sense. The Black Arrows had been one of the most famous and spectacular teams in the RAF's history so they chose to call the new team the arrows as well.

The Red Arrows were formed officially on 1 March 1965 at their new base of RAF Fairford in Gloucestershire. Fairford was an ideal location being close to the Central Flying School at Little Rissington but virtually unused

BELOW A huge crowd watching an early Red Arrows display

by any other aircraft. Previously display teams had scheduled their practices between training flights and other activities taking place on a busy operational airfield. Now they had the sky to themselves and could practice as often as was required to work up and perfect their routine.

WHY HAVE A TEAM?

Display teams always had two main aims. To entertain the public and to show off the RAF's front line aircraft at their best. However they had always been picked from squadrons and had only been able to display sporadically.

In 1965 the Red Arrows were set up as a separate operation to be run in the same way as a squadron. They had their own engineers and ground crew and even their own team manager, thirty one year old Squadron Leader Dick Storer who had flown Hunters before converting to Vulcans. As well as administering the team Storer flew the spare aircraft to air displays and then commentated for the crowd. Back at Fairford Storer had an even more important role as far as Lee Jones was concerned. He would stand on the air-

field and watch every practice display. Afterwards he was the team's severest critic if criticism was needed. Similar to Lee Jones he wanted perfection from the team! They were dedicated to aerobatics and formation flying. They were to show off the RAF at its best, to showcase the Gnat as a British-built trainer and to entertain the public both at home and abroad. The whole team was all determined to be the best.

SMOKE ON GO!

The early 1960s was a difficult period for the RAF. After years of spiralling costs to maintain a nuclear deterrent and ever more complex frontline aircraft the government's budget of 1964 proposed huge defence cuts. Aircraft carriers were scrapped and the advanced warplane of the future, TSR2, was cancelled. The RAF needed good publicity and some good news!

That first year the Red Arrows displayed many times at airfields and cities in six countries. Their first display introduced the team to the press at Little Rissington on 6 May 1965. Three days later they performed their first public display during the French Air

Force's National Air Day at Clermont Ferrand in France. Just a few days later, on May 15, the British public got their first view of the team at Biggin Hill.

Their display was broken into three distinct sections. The seven aircraft flew a flypast before several minutes of tight formations which changed at the top of each loop. The team then broke into two sections, one of five and two soloists who became the 'synchro pair.' Pilots Henry Prince and Bill Loverseed formed the 'Synchro pair' and thrilled the crowds with knife edge passes. It seemed to the crowd as though the two aircraft were passing inches apart at a combined speed of over 600mph. When the team reformed for a final flypast and either departed or landed the crowd knew they had watched the best the RAF had to offer.

The new team received immediate acclaim from the press and public alike. According to Flight magazine 150,000 people watched "the Gnats put on a fine 15 minute sequence" and commented that "very impressive was the team's downward bomb-burst with smoke on which two aircraft then superimposed an upward burst". Such was the impact in that first season that in the spring of 1966 the team were awarded the Royal Aero Club's major award, the Britannia Trophy, for meritorious service as an aerobatic team.

No-one wanted to leave the team and the threat of removal would have been the ultimate punishment but the team only stayed together for that one year. Almost all the pilots were given new postings at the end of the season. Just Ray Hanna and Henry Prince remained to bring on the next group of pilots wanting to wear the red flying suits.

In their first year the Red Arrows had been able to combine all the skills and disciplines of close flying with great entertainment for the crowds. Lee Jones' professionalism meant that he was concerned about every small part of the display from the quality of the flying and the closeness of the formations to positioning in the sky. In his opinion if the crowd had to look too near to the sun to see the aircraft then he had failed to create the perfect display. He wanted to mix the professional close flying with the spectacular formations that thrilled the crowds and this had to be done whatever the location or weather. He set the standard that future leaders would follow.

Chapter 4

The Gnat Years

THE RAY HANNA TEAMS

Their triumphant award-winning first year ensured that the Red Arrows continued into their second year. Ray Hanna was promoted to Squadron Leader and took command for 1966. The popularity of the team as crowd pullers meant Hanna was to lead the team at many more displays than the previous year. They performed all over Europe travelling to Norway, Germany, France, Belgium and Italy in between their UK displays. Later in the year the team performed in Malta and Cyprus before flying on to Jordan to display in front of King Hussein, himself a pilot.

For the 1966 season the team added two more pilots but they flew as reserves as the number of aircraft stayed at seven. However 8 July 1966 proved to be a milestone for the team. Displaying in front of the Duke of Edinburgh at Little Rissington they flew nine aircraft for the first time. Two days later they flew nine again at Pescara in Italy but it was to be 6 August before a British crowd were able to see all nine display during a show at RAF Brawdy in South Wales.

Having nine pilots but only flying a team of seven proved to be a problem. What were the two spares to do for most of the season? As understudies they had to be proficient in every other pilot's position. The extensive and intensive practice required meant that these two reserves were even better trained than the main seven but then they would get dissatisfied at being left out of the team.

ABOVE Red Arrows Gnats at Little Rissington in April 1966

So for 1968 the team was permanently increased to nine. In that same year they flew the Diamond Nine for the first time which has become the team's trademark ever since.

The process of putting together a routine was not the work of a moment. Ray Hanna naturally seemed to know what would look visually stunning to the crowd but many hours of discussion on the ground were needed before formations were tried in the air. What looked good in the air may not have the same impact from the ground so Dick Storer as team manager was vital in giving his impression and opinion.

A new routine would start with one or two aircraft at a time slowly building from the leader outwards until all the aircraft were involved. In the air the leader was king and only his voice would be heard in bursts of RT, giving notice to the other pilots when formations should change and smoke should be on. The leader's role became so important that throughout the team's

THE GNAT YEARS

ABOVE Red Arrows Gnat line-up at Biggin Hill in 1968

FAR RIGHT Seven of the team climbing in a formation called Leader's Benefit at Edinburgh in 1971

history whenever he is sick or unavailable the team does not fly.

In 1966 the Red Arrows performed at their first Farnborough Air Show. It was an important year for Farnborough as it was the first time overseas aircraft were allowed at the show as long as they used British engines or major British components. The rapid contraction of British aircraft manufacturing in the late 1950s and early 1960s had left the organisers with no choice. The only truly British new aircraft at the shows was the Britten-Norman Islander while manufacturers such as Piaggio, Fiat and Aermacchi from Italy and the Franco German joint venture, Transall, brought their new aircraft for the first time.

Multi aircraft displays had always been part of Farnborough and the RAF were not going to have it all their own way. The Royal Navy still had a formidable array of aircraft and they provided displays by Fairey Gannets, Wessex helicopters, Blackburn Buccaneers and an amazing ten Sea Vixens. However the Red Arrows introduced a new four-ship synchro display and the team produced a flawless performance.

Towards the end of the 1966 season the team moved from their base at Fairford to Kemble just a few miles

THE GNAT YEARS

ABOVE & FAR RIGHT
The Red Arrows
displaying in 1970

away. With its long runway Fairford was to become a Transport Command airfield. Kemble had been the headquarters of the Air Transport Auxiliary during the Second World war providing pilots for ferrying operations all over the country. It would now stay as the base for the Red Arrows team throughout its time on Gnats and continue after the Hawks had replaced them.

Over the next two years the team developed into a fully fledged internationally recognised team. Despite the grounding of all the RAF Gnats early in 1967 due to structural problems the team displayed for the first time in the USA and the Paris Air Show in France. 1969, however, was a difficult year.

After three years in command Ray Hanna was replaced by previous team member Squadron Leader Tim Nelson. However a mix of bad luck and bad weather conspired to make his a short command.

The year started well as the team was given permanent status. This meant that there was no requirement for annual consideration by the Ministry of Defence whether they could afford the Red Arrows for another year. In March the team suffered its first fatality when new member Jerry Bowler flew into some trees during a routine display practice at Kemble. This tragedy, combined with lack of practice time due to appalling winter and spring weather, conspired to ruin the team's preparations. Concerned by the time needed to get the team up to scratch the authorities reappointed Ray Hanna as leader for one further season.

Ray Hanna flew with the Red Arrows for five years and led them for four completing his command at the end of the 1969 season. In recognition of his leadership he had been awarded the Britannia trophy for 1968.

UNDER THREAT

The next two years was perhaps the worst time for the Red Arrows. A succession of crashes and accidents killed four pilots and caused injuries to three

THE GNAT YEARS

ABOVE Ground crew working on the Red Arrows Gnats at RAF Finningley in 1978. Note their Hercules at the far end unloading equipment

more. One of the injured was 1970 team leader Squadron Leader Dennis Hazell who ejected safely after an engine failure. His injuries meant he had to give up the leadership of the 1971 team being replaced by first year pilot Bill Loverseed.

The most serious incident in the history of the team occurred in January 1971. Red Arrows Gnats had suffered a number of engine failures and Training Command decided to monitor their aircraft engines compared to other Gnats in the RAF. This meant that a second pilot had to sit in the back seat during training flights. The synchro pair were practicing a close passing manoeuvre called 'Roulette' when their wings touched. At low level the pilots had no chance of survival even though one ejected. Pilots Euan Perreaux and

John Haddock were killed along with their back seaters Colin Armstrong and John Lewis.

The loss of five aircraft in just thirteen months led to an inquiry and a serious likelihood the team would be disbanded. The two remaining pilots from the 1970 team, including Bill Loverseed, together with the three new pilots and further volunteers reformed as a seven ship team with a solo rather than a synchro pair. This revised formation was approved and they flew a safe and crowd-pleasing 1971 season.

The next few years saw the Red Arrows enhance their already impressive reputation. They toured the USA and Canada for the first time in 1972. Their first displays of the tour were performed in front of enormous crowds of 1.5 million at the 1972 Transpo

Exhibition in Washington. In 1973 the crowd in Lisbon was even bigger. 650,000 watched a single Red Arrows display, a record that stood for many years. 1973 was also the year the team flew 100 displays for the first time.

1975 was their tenth anniversary and was flown by a team made up of three experienced pilots and six newcomers.

It was also the final year in which only flying instructors were chosen as pilots for the team. Recruiting was opened up to all qualified pilots as long as they had completed at least one operational tour and flown 1,500 hours.

Selection of new pilots really started in December when a signal from the team invited volunteers to apply. By August there were always thirty to fifty names but that list was whittled down until perhaps eight or ten remained. The remaining pilots were given a flying test and a stringent interview after which the final two or three were chosen for the following year's team. A tour was, and still is, three years. The excitement of the new job sustained the pilots through the first two years but by

BELOW A tight formation at Farnborough in 1978

ABOVE: LEFT The synchro pair begin the 'Heart Loop' in 1975   RIGHT The team flies the Wineglass formation

BELOW: LEFT The Red Arrows in Big Nine formation   RIGHT The team breaks as they approach the crowd

BELOW A Red Arrows Gnat landing at St Athan after completing displays for the team in 1979

the last few months of the third year, and with more than 300 displays, and more than treble that in training flights, under their belt it was easy to understand that three years was enough.

There has never been any special gadget to keep aircraft in formation. It has always been the eyes and concentration of the pilots. In the early years a display ran no more than seventeen minutes. By the mid 1970s it was up to twenty-one minutes. Now the display runs closer to thirty minutes and there are often flypasts to and from displays. That level of intensity is hard work and is draining on even the most mentally and physically fit pilot. On completion of their tour with the Red Arrows most of the pilots are pleased to return to the normal world of the RAF.

REDS AT RIAT

In 1977 two new manoeuvres were created to celebrate the Queen's Silver Jubilee. That year the team took part in a flypast for the Queen's birthday and appeared at the Silver Jubilee Review. 1977 was also the year in which they completed their first 1,000 displays.

This was on 26 June at the International Air Tattoo, an annual air show close to the hearts of the Red Arrows.

The Air Tattoo began at North Weald in 1971, organised by Paul Bowen,

Tim Prince and Sir Denis Crowley-Milling. Crowley-Milling had been a Battle of Britain fighter pilot flying in 242 Squadron under the command of legendary ace, Douglas Bader. Now as controller of the Royal Air Force Benevolent Fund he looked for new ways to raise funding for the charity.

The Tattoo was a small affair to begin with but as reputations grew so did the flying display until, more than forty years later, it is now recognised as the greatest military air show in the world. In 1996 it gained the Royal status and has been known as the Royal International Air Tattoo since then. For many years the tattoo has been at RAF Fairford, the team's first home, and it is a place that has created many unique flypasts, most of which feature the Red Arrows. The team first displayed at Fairford in 1974 and they have missed very few since then.

Over the years the early July diary has been automatically filled in with the few days the team spends at Fairford. It is one of the most important fund raising events in the calendar and it is also where display teams get together. Every year the skies of Gloucestershire are filled with teams from Europe and the United States and increasingly from the Middle East and Far East.

THE END OF THE GNAT

The Folland Gnat had never been the easiest aircraft to fly and maintain and the stresses of constant displaying and practicing meant that almost every year one or more of the team's aircraft needed replacing. The flying schools were suffering the same problems and so the RAF began to look for a replacement.

The successful story of the development of the Hawk is told elsewhere in this book but when the time came to change the Red Arrows had to say goodbye to their Gnats that had given such great service for fifteen seasons. By 1979 the team had changed considerably from the one that first performed for the press in May 1965. Three of the original aircraft, serial numbers XR540, XR991 and XR987, were still flying in the final season but many others had come and gone in between mainly due to fatigue or crashes. The colour scheme, while still Post Office red, now included the words Royal Air Force on the nose. The team's original transport for the ground crew, the Armstrong Whitworth Argosy, had been replaced with a C-130 Hercules. And perhaps the biggest change of all was in the training and preparation for each season. That year the Red Arrows finished their work up by taking their Gnats to Cyprus during the spring for an intensive final few weeks. This started a tradition that still exists today. Every March the team flies to RAF Akrotiri and uses the clear blue Mediterranean skies to hone their routine to perfection.

The Red Arrows received their new Hawks between August and November 1979 while they were still displaying their Gnats. On 15 September the team flew two displays in front of the public before a final display at RAF Valley in North Wales, the home of 4FTS.

With one of the new Hawks on the ground at RAF Kemble, the team performed a precision flypast, their last act before converting to their new aircraft.

BELOW Two of the Red Arrows Gnats in storage at RAF Cosford in 1982

Chapter 5

The Hawk

For 35 years the Hawk trainer has been the aircraft flown by the Red Arrows. Painted in their distinctive red scheme with white flashes underside the nine aircraft are instantly recognisable.

The Hawks were delivered to the Red Arrows in late 1979. The team converted to them through the winter and worked up their new display routine for the summer season of 1980. They replaced the original Gnats as flown by the Red Arrows since the beginning of the team in 1965.

The team had always flown the primary jet trainer employed by the RAF so, as the Gnat was being phased out and replaced by the Hawk it was the right time for the team to change aircraft.

THE DEVELOPMENT OF THE HAWK

The story of the Hawk is one of problem-free design and development from the experienced team at Hawker Siddeley Aviation based at the iconic and historic Hawker building in Kingston in Surrey. Many of them had worked through the Hunter and Harrier programmes and some of the Gnat development team had joined them when Folland was merged into Hawker Siddeley in 1959.

The team, led by ex-Folland designer Gordon Hodson, knew there would only be one new trainer for the RAF and it would stay in service for many years so it would be a valuable contract to win. A combat capability was to

be attached to the new aircraft which would increase the chances of international success as well.

The original plan was for the two-seat variant of the Jaguar to take on the role but it proved to be too expensive and complex for fast jet training. The only two seat aircraft that were bought were used for converting pilots on to the Jaguar alone.

The specification from the Ministry of Defence came in 1970. Hawker Siddeley, pre-empting the requirement, had started on their design as a private venture in 1968 and the RAF had worked closely with the design team. Almost unique in British aviation the Ministry of Defence placed an order for

ABOVE The iconic Hawker building in Kingston in Surrey where all the Hawker aircraft were designed

LEFT Sir Sydney Camm, the great designer who was responsible for so many Hawker aircraft including the Fury, Hurricane, Tempest, Typhoon, Hunter and P.1127

175 Hawks before the aircraft had been tested or even flown for the first time!

Hawker Siddeley test pilot Duncan Simpson flew the Hawk for the first time on 21 August 1974, close to the fifteenth anniversary of the first flight of the Gnat. He found it to be everything that the plans said it would be.

What Simpson had flown was a stable, comfortable aircraft. It had a good field of vision which was vital for a trainee pilot, and it handled well within the spinning and stalling requirements of the specification. Equally important

it was cost effective to build and to maintain.

Just a few days later Simpson took the aircraft to Farnborough for the air show. In awful weather he flew it throughout the eight days of the 1974 show.

Now started the serious testing and development. The serviceability record proved to be remarkable. As with the experimental period the testing went according to plan. The first production aircraft for the RAF went ahead on time and the Hawk entered service in April

ABOVE The Hawker Hunter Mk.3 prototype WB188 in which Neville Duke broke the World Speed Record in 1953

FAR LEFT The final production Hurricane "The Last of the Many" paraded through the streets of Kingston in 1944

1976 barely eighteen months after the first flight.

NEW TRAINERS FOR THE RAF

The Hawk provided exactly what the Royal Air Force needed at that time. The job of the advanced jet trainer was to transition pilots from their basic jet training on the Jet Provost to whichever was to be their front line strike aircraft. As cockpits became more complex then the training needed to provide that level of complexity. The Hawk achieved this by providing a similar cockpit layout to

ABOVE XX154 at the SBAC Air Show at Farnborough after just nine previous flights

BELOW XX157, the third production Hawk being constructed in the factory at Kingston in 1975

THE HAWK

ABOVE: LEFT G-HAWK ZA101 - the Hawk used as a development aircraft for various export versions
RIGHT The 4FTS line-up of Hawks at RAF Valley in 1980

BELOW Hawk 63 built for the United Arab Emirates Air Force

THE HAWK

ABOVE Hawk 103 export version built as a fighter trainer for the Royal Air Force of Oman

BELOW: LEFT Canadian Hawk Mk115 RIGHT Goshawk T-45 fully carrier-capable version used to train US Navy pilots, a joint venture between McDonnell Douglas and British Aerospace

ABOVE Goshawk T-45A basic trainer version for the US Navy

that of the front line aircraft of the time.

The aircraft was powered by an engine built under a joint venture between Britain and France. The Rolls Royce / Turbomeca Adour 151-01 engine was chosen because of its reliability, fuel efficiency and most of all because it had been tested successfully in the Anglo French SEPECAT Jaguar.

The Hawk could climb fast and could go supersonic in a dive and had great endurance. All in all the Royal Air Force had a terrific new jet training aircraft that would last them well beyond the end of the 20th Century.

IN RAF SERVICE

For five years from 1976 the RAF's new Hawks were delivered to training schools all over the country. First to get them was No.4 Flying Training School which had been established originally in 1921 in Egypt and had moved to Iraq and Southern Rhodesia before transfer to the UK for the first time at Middleton St George in County Durham in 1954. In 1960 the school moved to its current home at RAF Valley on the island of Anglesey in North Wales. For more than fifty years generations of RAF fast

ABOVE Mock-up of the Goshawk T-45 for the Farnborough Air Show in 1984

jet pilots have graduated from 4 FTS and gone on to fly everything from the Lightning and Hunter to the Tornado and Typhoon.

Nowadays 4FTS provides a 28 to 30 week course of both flying and weapons training, All the flying elements of the courses are based around the Hawk. 208(R) Squadron at Valley provides all the flying training while 19(R) Squadron, famous as the first ever Spitfire Squadron, provides the weapons training. At the end of the course qualified pilots are ready to move on to their frontline aircraft.

By 1982 all 175 Hawk T.Mk1 aircraft had been delivered to flying training schools and tactical weapons units. The following year the MoD contracted British Aerospace to modify the wings of 88 of the Hawks to T.Mk.1A standard so that they could carry Sidewinder air-to-air missiles. Among those aircraft were the ones that had been flown by the Red Arrows for the previous three years.

HAWKS FOR THE RED ARROWS

In the late 70s the Gnats flown by the

Red Arrows were beginning to show their age. Three of their aircraft had been with the team for 15 years and had flown more than 1,000 displays. It was time to change over to the RAF's latest jet trainer. In November 1979 the Commandant of the Central Flying School took delivery of the ninth aircraft that would fly with the team. A reserve aircraft was delivered later but the Red Arrows were now ready to work up their routine during the winter of 1979 / 80.

These aircraft were similar in every way to those flown by the training schools apart from two changes. First they were fitted with slightly uprated engines, the Adour 151-02, which gives a faster response to the pilots giving them even more precision for their manoeuvres. Second they were fitted with smoke pods. Diesel mixed with coloured dye is pumped into the jet exhaust which delivers the red, white or blue smoke used in the displays.

Despite accidents and aircraft fatigue a number of the original aircraft delivered in 1979 are still being flown by the team, a testament to the endurance and ruggedness of the type.

HAWKS FOR EXPORT

As soon as the Hawk was established with the RAF Hawker Siddeley was on the search for export orders. A major tour with the Red Arrows in 1981 helped bring orders from the Middle East and countries all over the world found the Hawk to be exactly what they needed for training their pilots.

Finland, Kenya and Indonesia were the first customers for the Hawk 50, the initial export version. In the early 1980s the next version, the Hawk 60, attracted orders from the Middle East as well as South Korea, Zimbabwe and Switzerland.

Into the 1990s and the Hawk 100, a weapons trainer with advanced avionics, secured more interest from the Middle East, including Oman for the first time, and Malaysia together with the first orders from the North American continent when Canada ordered what would become the CT-155 Hawk.

21ST CENTURY HAWK

In 2014 the Hawk is still the most successful jet trainer aircraft in the world. Almost 1,000 have been sold and they are in service with thirteen countries. Perhaps the most important overseas agreement is with the United States. America buys from America most of the time. Boeing and Lockheed Martin are two of the biggest aircraft manufacturers in the world and it is unusual to see that stranglehold being broken by a foreign manufacturer.

In 1978 British Aerospace, recently formed from the merger of Hawker Siddeley and BAC, together with McDonnell Douglas jointly developed the T-45 Goshawk as a carrier-borne jet trainer for the US Navy. 125 T-45As were ordered and now, more than thirty years later, the T-45C is still providing advanced training to US naval aviators.

FAR LEFT: TOP Hawk XX159 in 30 Years colours, 2004

BOTTOM The Red Arrows Hawks ready for their display at Binbrook in 1982

Chapter 6

Red Arrows - The Hawk Years

THE HAWK'S FIRST YEAR

The leader during the crossover period from Gnats to Hawks was Squadron Leader Brian Hoskins. He had flown two tours on Hunters and one as a flying instructor on Jet Provosts at Manby. He had been a member of the JP display team, The Macaws, leading the team in 1970 and 71. The team was not named after the parrot but a mix of Ma from Manby and CAW from the College of Air Warfare.

Hoskins was selected for the Red Arrows towards the end of 1974 spending two years with the team in 1975 and 1976 as one of the synchro pair. He converted on to Buccaneers and spent a tour on 208 Squadron before returning to the Red Arrows as team leader for the 1979 season.

Hoskins converted to the Hawk in the spring of 1979 and was instrumental in making sure the aircraft was set up correctly for display and formation flying. There were two main advantages flying the Hawk over the Gnat. The first was the instant response the aircraft gave to changes in speed and braking allowing tighter and quicker formation changes. The second was the range and endurance which substantially improved the team's ability to tour abroad and to do multiple displays in the same day without having to land and refuel.

On 15 November 1979 the ninth Hawk was handed over to the Red Arrows in a ceremony at the British Aerospace plant at Bitteswell in Leicestershire. The team now set about creating their display for the 1980 season.

ABOVE The Red Arrows in their Gnats fly over the Team's first Hawk in August 1979

The aircraft were still bright red, Signal rather than Post Office this time, but the white flashes changed, new ones being painted on the underside, and a new badge was added. This was the first time a badge had been allowed for the team and it featured a Diamond Nine formation with the word Éclat which means Brilliance.

Intensive practice all winter was followed by the usual trip to Cyprus where they flew their first two displays on the new aircraft in cloudless skies. Their debut in the UK was cancelled due to appalling weather and on one of their early displays, at Brighton on 17 May, Steve Johnson, flying as part of the synchro pair, sliced part of his wing off on the mast of a yacht. Johnson ejected safely and maybe all the bad luck for that season was now behind them.

In truth the 1980 display routine was very similar to that of previous seasons. The one difference was that the

ABOVE Red Arrows and Thunderbirds pilots line up, 1983

Hawk's abilities meant that the whole routine could be flown well within the strict limits put on by the Civil Aviation Authority. This is an area of six nautical miles radius from the datum or centre of the display and extends upwards to 8,000 feet. It is essential that the team stays within those limits but equally important that other air traffic stays out. Nine pilots fully concentrating on flying just a few feet from each other find it almost impossible to take notice of other aircraft that may be flying into their restricted airspace. Every year there are incidents of microlights, gliders and light aircraft straying into the team's space disrupting the displays and creating safety hazards.

THE 1980s

After a successful first year 1981 started with a major tour of the Middle East where they worked closely with British Aerospace getting international orders for the Hawk. This was followed by a full season of displays including flypasts for the wedding of the Prince of Wales and Princess Diana and the opening of the Humber bridge as well as further overseas trips to Denmark, Germany and Japan.

At the end of the 1981 season Brian Hoskins left to command RAF Brawdy flying Hawks and Hunters before becoming station commander

RED ARROWS - THE HAWK YEARS

ABOVE One of three brand new Hawks taking off for their first practice sortie at Kemble in 1979

BELOW: LEFT Squadron Leader Brian Hoskins and his eight pilots line-up for the first official photos of the 1980 team and their new Hawks
RIGHT Six Hawks in the hangar at Kemble in 1980

ABOVE: LEFT VIPs and officials sit on the beach in Bahrain watching the Red Arrows display during the major Middle East tour in 1981
RIGHT A shot from the debut season for the Red Arrows after converting to Hawks. Displaying at Cosford in May 1980

BELOW The Red Arrows break at Cosford in 1982

ABOVE The classic trademark of the Red Arrows - The Diamond Nine

BELOW: LEFT The synchro pair thrill the crowd as they pass just a few feet from each other
RIGHT The Wineglass formation flown after crashes had reduced the team to a seven-ship formation in 1988

ABOVE The Red Arrows in Big Nine formation with two Spitfires at RIAT in 2005 commemorating the 60th anniversary of the end of the Second World War

at Akrotiri, the Cypriot base that played host to the Red Arrows every spring. He had seen the team integrate safely and successfully with the Hawk and had provided a platform for the future.

During the years from 1982 to 1984 the team was led by John Blackwell who had originally flown for the team as Red 5 as far back as 1975. He was a flying instructor before joining the Red Arrows for the first time then went on to fly Jaguars at RAF Coltishall for 54 Squadron. He then spent time in the

USA on an exchange posting flying A-10 Thunderbolts. He faced a tough three years in the job.

The first issue was the Falklands War in 1982. In the busiest year in the team's history the team included tribute flypasts to the servicemen who had fought and died in the South Atlantic. The second was preparing for a move of bases from Kemble to Scampton.

Kemble had been the home to the Red Arrows since September 1966 but after almost 17 years it was time to move on as Kemble was to became a maintenance facility for the United States Air Force.

Scampton in Lincolnshire had a history all of its own. A Lancaster bomber base during the war it was the home of 617 Squadron when they set out on the evening of 16 May 1943 to attack the great dams of western Germany. The exploits of the squadron and their commander, Guy Gibson, had gained them the nickname of the Dambusters. Post war Scampton became a base for Vulcan bombers carrying their Blue Steel nuclear weapons. Now, in the spring of 1983, it became the home of the Red Arrows as they returned from their Cyprus training. Just a few weeks later they were off on a massive tour of the United States.

Acting as ambassadors for Great Britain the team arrived at Andrews Air Force Base in Maryland near Washington DC and displayed in front of an enormous crowd, military chiefs and diplomats as well as the British Ambassador to the United States. Even the United States Air Force's official team, the Thunderbirds, agreed it was a fabulous performance and these rave reviews continued as they displayed across America.

The team returned at the end of May with a great reputation having flown for 400 hours and over 11,000 miles.

The next milestone in the team's history was their 2,000th display which was officially flown at Hurn during the Bournemouth air show in 1986 before they flew off on a marathon Far East tour.

The 1988 season started with a catastrophic few weeks when new team leader Squadron Leader Tim Miller and Red 2 Spike Newbery collided during a training sortie in November 1987. Ejecting from his smoke-filled cockpit Miller suffered back injuries but recovered in time for the start of the 1988 season. Newbery, however, broke his leg and had to be replaced in the team. Just a few weeks later on 22 January Neil MacLachlan was killed when he crashed practicing low level manoeuvres. Another aircraft was lost in June of 1988 and although the pilot ejected safely the team continued as a seven ship for the rest of the year.

Since their formation the Red Arrows had displayed many times in Germany and almost every year they had visited Ramstein Air Base. On 28 August, during a display, aircraft of the Italian Air Force display team, the Frecce Tricolori, collided. The resulting crashes and fireball created by spilled aviation fuel killed three pilots and 67 spectators making it the worst ever air show accident up to that time. 1988 was to be the Red Arrows last visit to Germany.

1989 was the Red Arrows silver jubilee and teams from all over Europe came to Scampton to celebrate.

INTO THE 90s

The USSR was the latest new venue when the team made their first historic visit in June 1990 just months after the Berlin wall had come down and the Cold War ended. The tour was very successful but it would be a further 22 years before the team would return

The team reached 3,000 displays in 1995 but that same year Scampton was closed for economic reasons. With no permanent home to go to at the end of the season the team embarked on what would be their longest tour ever. Their unprecedented five month odyssey took in South Africa, Australia, many countries in the Far East and Middle East and the team was away from September

until the following February. When they returned they found their new home would be RAF Cranwell.

It must have felt like they had come home. Cranwell was the home of the Central Flying School and the team shared the base with the CFS Bulldogs, Jetstreams and Dominies. However Cranwell did not work for the Red Arrows. The sheer volume of air traffic during training sorties meant that the team had to use Scampton for winter training and eventually at the end of 2000 the team returned to Scampton permanently.

2000 AND BEYOND

In 2004 the Red Arrows marked their 40th season with a private celebration at RAF Cranwell and another triumphant display year.

In the 10 years since then there have been many special occasions; flypasts with new and retiring RAF aircraft, tours to all corners of the globe, the London 2012 Olympics and the Queen's Diamond Jubilee celebrations.

In 2009 the first woman to fly with the team was announced. Flight Lieutenant Kirsty Moore had flown a tour on the

Tornado GR4 and taught student pilots on the Hawk. She took part in her first display at the beginning of the 2010 season.

However there have been further tragedies for the team and 2011 was a particularly sad year. Within a few weeks of each other two of the team were killed. Jon Egging crashed after the Bournemouth Air Show in August and soon after Sean Cunningham was ejected from his stationary Hawk at Scampton. These deaths led to the team displaying with seven aircraft throughout the 2012 season.

Chapter 7

Red Arrows – A Year in the Life

THE NEW BOYS ARRIVE

The Red Arrows year starts in the previous October when the new pilots for the team are announced. Traditionally the team brings in two or three new pilots every year, and their tour with the team lasts three years. Hundreds apply and the expectations are high. The best are shortlisted and through a series of rigorous tests and interviews the final pilots are selected. The lucky few will have at least five or six years' experience flying fast jets and will have had at least one operational tour. The arrival of new pilots refreshes the whole team and adds a new spirit to the existing experienced members.

WINTER TRAINING

The winter training schedule is tough as the pilots fly three times each day five days a week, not flying as a nine ship formation at this point but in twos

and threes slowly bringing together the elements of the following year's display routine. At the same time the ground crew are hard at work giving all the famous red Hawks a thorough overhaul ready for the year ahead. Stripped down and almost rebuilt from scratch some of the Red Arrows' Hawks have been flown by the team since the team switched to them in the autumn of 1979.

The responsibility for creating the routine sits with the leader. There are many proven manoeuvres and seldom is there something new after nearly fifty years of displays unless something special is created for an anniversary or special celebration. The routine needs to work for everyone in the crowd and as that sometimes tops 100,000 it's not easy. The RAF has always erred on the side of the family audience rather than the aviation enthusiast. Keep the aircraft in front of the crowd all the time even if it means that huge spectacular break has to be left out. Keep in what people want to see and add a few things that they don't expect. There are so many ways to make it work and all leaders have previously spent years in

ABOVE The 1994 Red Arrows taxy to the runway at the International Air Tattoo at Fairford

FAR LEFT Red Arrows Hawk XX233 which crashed after Red 6 pilot Mike Ling ejected over Crete in 2010. He was in a collision with Red 7 Dave Montenegro who landed his aircraft safely

ABOVE One of the 'flying circus' of ground crew who fly with the aircraft to all displays

FAR RIGHT The Snowbirds from 431 Squadron RCAF, Canada's National air display team, flying their CT-114 Tutors

the team so know what to do.

By March the full routine is coming together but weather often gets in the way of finding perfection during early Spring. Five months of training now ends with five intensive weeks. Every year the team travels to RAF Akrotiri in Cyprus, Britain's largest air force base in the Mediterranean.

They split their time between Cyprus and Crete. The team spends virtually every working moment together, flying, briefing, reviewing and flying again. And of course some socialising and downtime on the beaches of southern Cyprus.

Accidents do happen and in 2010 the synchro pair touched wings as they practiced one of their high speed passing manoeuvres over Crete. Red 7 Dave Montenegro managed to land his Hawk safely but Red 6 Mike Ling had to eject at less than 1,000ft. Suffering minor injuries he was unable to fly with the team for the rest of that season. It meant that a new pilot, Pablo O'Grady, had to be brought in. O'Grady had flown a tour with the Red Arrows before and had been in the synchro pair with the 2010 leader Ben Murphy. It also meant a few early air displays had to

ABOVE The US Navy's display team, The Blue Angels, flying their F/A-18 Hornets

be cancelled. Mike Ling recovered and eventually became the team's manager and Red 10.

The last few days of the spring trip are vital to the whole display season ahead as one of the highest ranking RAF officers has to watch the display and give the final public display approval.

To this point the team has spent all winter wearing standard green RAF flying suits. Now, with final approval confirmed, the team can start to wear their famous red flying suits. It's a proud moment for both new and experienced pilots alike.

INTO THE SEASON

The team returns to their base at RAF Scampton at the end of their five weeks in Cyprus. There they are welcomed by their families. It's a hard time for them. Most of the pilots are in their thirties and have young children but a three year posting to the Red Arrows is more than a full time job, in particular during the summer when the team stays away from base a lot.

Now starts the season the team has spent all winter training for, four to five months during which they will fly at least sixty displays at air shows and other events at home and abroad.

Every year their schedule is different. There are the regular events and major air shows where the Red Arrows always appear but new dates get added to the diary all the time. That first show can be a shock to the new pilots. All those weeks of concentrating on perfecting the routine and suddenly there are tens of thousands of people watching your every move.

In 2013 one of the first shows after leaving Cyprus was for the 60th anniversary of the Patrouille de France, the French Air Force's display team, on 25 and 26 May at Salon de Provence, the Patrouille's home base. This was followed by displays at events as diverse as the TT races on the Isle of Man, Scarborough air show and the British Grand Prix at Silverstone.

BELOW The opposing solos from the US Air Force's display team, the Thunderbirds, flying their F-16 Fighting Falcons in a knife edge pass

ABOVE The Red Arrows lined up at RIAT at Fairford in 2003

A NORTH AMERICAN TRIP

On occasions the team takes on an extensive overseas tour and in 2008 they undertook a major journey. Invited to display at the Quebec Air Show held at the Jean Lesage International Airport to celebrate the 400th anniversary of the founding of the city, the Red Arrows had to deal with a major logistical exercise. The red-painted Hawks do not hold large fuel tanks so a 4,000 mile trip to Canada meant seven stops and a four day trip on the way out. Refuelling stops in Scotland, Iceland and into the arctic circle in Greenland were needed before landfall in Canada and further stops before finally reaching Quebec.

The show seemed more like a stand off between four of the World's premier display teams. The USAF F-16 team, the Thunderbirds, were there as were the US Navy's Blue Angels with their F/A-18 Hornets. Hosts were the Royal Canadian Air Force Snowbirds flying their Canadair CT-114 Tutors. All teams put on their very best shows but it could be said that the American and Canadian teams were impressed by the Red Arrows' prowess!

MID SUMMER

The middle of the summer is always an important part of the season. The major RAF air show at RAF Waddington just south of Lincoln is almost home territory and in 2013 it was another milestone for the team as they flew their 4,500th display.

A week later is RIAT, the annual Royal International Air Tattoo, at RAF Fairford in Gloucestershire. Fairford was the original home of the Red Arrows when they were formed in 1965

BELOW Four Red Arrow T.1s during the Royal International Air Tattoo, RAF Fairford, Gloucestershire, July 2006

ABOVE The Red Arrows fly escort to the new European-developed Airbus A400M Atlas transport aircraft for the Royal Air Force at RIAT in 2013

and therefore holds a special place in the hearts of the team. It's also the place where they have flown many 'firsts' with other aircraft. 2006 was the 40th anniversary of the VC10 in service with the RAF. A specially painted aircraft from 101 Squadron at Brize Norton flew with the Red Arrows in celebration. In 2013 the team flew a spectacular formation with the Airbus A400M Atlas which will be the RAF's new transport aircraft. It's these extra formations and flypasts that have made RIAT unique and very special for over forty years.

In his role as Red 10 Squadron Leader Graeme Bagnall was team manager, commentator, spare Hawk pilot and even checked the weather conditions for the team. Seen here at Bournemouth in Dorset in 2009

Every other year is Farnborough International, no longer in its old traditional September slot for a spectacular ending to the display season. It's the week after RIAT in the middle of July. Having the two air shows back to back means that both get the best that overseas has to offer. The Red Arrows first flew at Farnborough in 1966. Forty years later they flew in formation with the enormous Airbus A380 airliner when it visited a UK air show for the first time.

Its an intensive time with air shows and flypasts all over Britain so at the mid season point they take a break. A week away for the pilots and engineers who travel with them. That gives the Scampton-based engineers a chance to work on the aircraft and get them in tiptop shape for the rest of the season. It also gives the pilots a chance to say hello to their families but then it's back to flying again.

It's August and the summer holidays are in full swing. The team displays over beaches and coastlines packed with holidaymakers. Blackpool, Bournemouth, Eastbourne, Minehead, Torbay, Clacton, the seaside gets very familiar to the pilots.

THE SEASON ENDING

Now the children have gone back to school and the final air shows of the year are on the calendar. The main Duxford Air Show is a big two-day event in early September. In 2013 it was the final ever Leuchars Air Show at the Scottish RAF base after 67 years and, of course, the Red Arrows were the headliners.

By this time the new pilots for next year have moved to Scampton and are learning about the pace of life they will enjoy for the next three years. They've known about it for a few months but nothing can really prepare them. It's completely different to a regular RAF posting. Intensive training and so much more flying. Overseas trips and the spotlight is always on them.

Not only are they planning every display and every transit as well as concentrating on every individual display.

There's the PR, meeting the press and the VIPs wherever they go. They walk the crowdline, handing out brochures, signing autographs and answering hundreds of questions.

The three pilots due to leave are winding down and preparing for their next posting. At the end of the season

BELOW The traditional October display by the Red Arrows at their home base at Scampton in Lincolnshire in 1989

FAR LEFT Nine Red Arrow Hawk T.1s in formation with Airbus A.380-800, Farnborough, U.K., July 2006

RED ARROWS - A YEAR IN THE LIFE

IMAGES
Three dramatic formations during the traditional October display by the Red Arrows at their home base at Scampton in Lincolnshire in 1989

RED ARROWS - A YEAR IN THE LIFE

BELOW Red Arrows at rest. The aircraft are looked after by the ground crew after another long season in 2008

in the UK there are regularly a few trips abroad. Maybe the annual Malta Air Show or somewhere else in the Mediterranean. It could also mean a major overseas tour as the team regularly visit the Middle East and have toured all over the world.

Every three years the leader changes so there is an even more intense period when the team is flying displays, integrating the new pilots, saying goodbye to the old ones, learning the methods of the new boss and thinking about the new routine for next year. And then they are into winter training again. There's never a dull moment for a Red Arrows pilot.

IMAGE The Red Arrows fly over the Malaysian jungle during their gruelling 1986 tour of the Far East

Chapter 8

Red Arrows - Flying the Flag

FAR RIGHT The Red Arrows in Tango formation

Ever since their formation one of the major roles for the Red Arrows has been flying the flag for Britain and British industry abroad.

When the Red Arrows received their new Hawks it was decided that there was nothing better than the world's best display team to help promote and sell this brand new British-built aircraft.

SELLING THE HAWK

In March 1981 a big banner announced "welcome to British Aerospace and the Red Arrows" as the partners travelled the Middle East hand in hand; the Red Arrows flying them and British Aerospace selling them!

The tour was only two weeks but in that time they transited via Cyprus to Dubai, Abu Dhabi, Sharjah and Bahrain before travelling on to Jordan for further displays. The British Defence Minister at that time was John Nott and it was reported that this triple attack of politics, industry and display had not only produced Hawk sales to the UAE but other defence equipment as well. Qatar had already ordered Alpha Jets from France but were excited by the Hawk. As they were already committed they showed interest in buying Rapier defensive missiles instead, also made by British Aerospace.

King Hussein of Jordan had always been an anglophile having been educated at Harrow and trained at the Royal Military Academy at Sandhurst. He was a skilled pilot and flew RAF

FAR RIGHT Feathered Arrow formation over the coastline in 1980

jets on many occasions. In 1955 he toured the Folland factory as the Gnat prototype was nearing completion and although Jordan never bought Gnats King Hussein stayed close to British industry. The Royal Jordanian Air Force had also bought Hunters and Vampires as well as a number of other British types.

When the Red Arrows arrived in Jordan at the end of March 1981 he was the first who wanted his photograph taken with the team and their new Hawk jets. His son was also pictured with them before they took off for a series of three displays that wowed the Jordanian hierarchy.

The trip had done its job and the Red Arrows would be taken along on many more occasions to help promote the aircraft.

TOURING THE WORLD

In 1986 the Red Arrows took a huge slice out of their summer diary to make a major tour to the Far East during June and July. For two weeks they displayed in Indonesia, Singapore, Brunei, Malaysia, Thailand, Bangladesh, India and Pakistan before stopping for a very

special display for the Deputy Prime Minister of Oman. They displayed three times in a single day in Jordan before flying to Egypt and on to Turkey.

Flight magazine reported that the team had flown 22 displays in 17 countries on that tour and that they had displayed in 'climates ranging from an Alpine summer to tropical monsoons.' At one show they flew in the hottest conditions they had ever experienced, a temperature of 45 degrees.

It's almost impossible to say what direct effect that tour had but it is significant that four of those countries, namely India, Indonesia, Malaysia and Oman bought almost 200 Hawks between them.

The Hawk has become the world's most successful jet trainer and the Red Arrows have been a huge part of the sales strategy.

The Middle East is a lucrative region for the sale of arms and aircraft and much effort is put into securing orders. While the Red Arrows actively assist in the sale of Hawks they can also be used almost as an incentive to support the sales of other aircraft. In November 2013 it was reported that the Red Arrows were being sent to Bahrain just

ABOVE All ten Red Arrows Hawks in formation behind their support Hercules over the deserts of Oman on their way back from their Far East tour of 1986

a few weeks after negotiations opened on the sale of Typhoon jets. At a display in Doha it was noted that the team flew a formation with the Typhoon. Its not all entertainment. There are times when business has to take the lead.

In their 50 years the Red Arrows have been to an amazing 54 countries but never have they been so far or been gone as long as their famous world tour of 1995 / 6. It started as a rumour of a visit to South Africa, the first time the team would have ever been there because of the political issues in the region. Even though Nelson Mandela had been released from jail and the apartheid regime removed it would be hard to justify the high cost of sending

ABOVE The team get into the spirit of their 1981 tour of the Middle East donning traditional Arab headdress while in the UAE

the team all that way.

As it turned out it wasn't just a trip to South Africa. By August of 1995 it was official. The team was going on a world tour taking in places such as Malaysia, Australia, Singapore and South Africa. They would be away for months and the £3,000,000 cost of the whole trip would be paid for by the British defence industry.

The tour started in September as the team flew straight from their planned shows in Turkey and Greece to the Middle East. The transit from there to South Africa took three days and seven stops as the aircraft had to refuel about every 800 miles.

At the airfield at Waterkloof, the South

IMAGE All ten pilots line up for an impromptu photo in front of their aircraft in Jordan in 1981

ABOVE The Red Arrows pictured with King Hussein of Jordan during the vital tour of the Middle East promoting the Hawk aircraft in 1981

African Air Force's most important base, they displayed in front of 27 Chiefs of Air Staffs from around the world all celebrating the SAAF's 75th anniversary. Trips to Natal and Zimbabwe ended the first half of the tour and the team returned to Scampton.

In November it was the turn of the Far East. A long transit through Malaysia, and shows in Darwin and Canberra, ended with the Red Arrows displaying over Sydney harbour on Australia Day in January 1996 watched by an estimated 1,500,000 people. The trip home took in Brunei, the Philippines, Singapore and Thailand before the team arrived at their new home at Cranwell on 21 February.

IMAGE The classic Diamond Nine formation flown over the desert of India in 1986

The Red Arrows displayed 42 times in 12 countries on that tour and probably deserved a rest but with a new season looming the new team got straight into training and to their credit and professionalism the first time they flew their new display was less than six weeks later.

The leader during the change of home base and the extended world tour was Squadron Leader John Rands who was awarded an OBE. In further tribute he was the subject of a This Is Your Life show for Thames Television later in 1996.

RUSSIAN DETENTE

In 1990 the Red Arrows visited Russia for the first time, not long after the Wall had come down. They displayed in Leningrad before two further shows at the British Trade Fair in Kiev. It was another 22 years before the team returned to Russia in 2012.

The highlight of that visit was two displays at the centenary celebrations for the Russian Air Force flown at the Zhukovsky Air Base 25 miles south of Moscow. That year the team were only flying seven aircraft after the tragedies of the previous year. All seven aircraft made the trip but the team had to fly a rather strange asymmetric 6-ship formation as one of the pilots had to return home.

A SPECIAL RELATIONSHIP

One of the most important links for the Red Arrows to maintain is with the United States. In their first 30 years the team only crossed the Atlantic three times but since then the trips have become more regular.

In 2008 the Red Arrows were guests at the annual AirPower show over Hampton Roads in Virginia. Based out of Langley Air Force Base their unique formation flown with the F.22 Raptor, flown by the F.22 demonstration pilot Major Paul Moga, was the highlight of the show. Reviewer Mike Sherba described the Red Arrows display as "some of the most incredible formation flying I have ever seen. Their precision and daring shows why they have earned their reputation for commitment and professionalism."

Even when they can't get to the United States the Red Arrows support their armed forces. On Independence Day 2013 the Red Arrows thrilled the crowds at RAF Feltwell in Norfolk, the

FAR LEFT An unforgettable picture of the Red Arrows over the Pyramids before displaying at the Egyptian Air Force Academy at Bilbeis on 17 July 1986

ABOVE The six-ship team flies over the Zhukovsky air base control tower during the air show celebrating the centenary of the Russian Air Force in 2012

setting for the families day from the US Air Force base at Lakenheath.

There are still many new adventures ahead for the team. They have never been to China and maybe Afghanistan will be on their future tour schedules. As long as they are in existence the Red Arrows will continue to travel the world, support British industry and perform their dazzling displays.

IMAGE The Red Arrows ended all their displays on the Middle East tour of 1981 with this spectacular Parasol Break

IMAGE Inch perfect the team flying the Diamond Bend during the annual air show at La Ferte Alais in France in 2009

Chapter 9

The Red Arrows have competition!

The British believe the Red Arrows are the best display team in the world. National identity plays a big part and a British team flying British-built aircraft around the world is always going to win the popular vote in the home country.

There are many people in other countries, however, who also think the Red Arrows are the best. Major tours to the Far East, the United States and the Middle East as well as regular displays at air shows and celebrations across Europe have created a huge fan base from all nations. There are also, however, a huge number of display teams elsewhere with air forces from more than thirty countries supporting national teams.

Some countries such as France and the United States have had teams for decades, promoting their own armed forces and nationally built aircraft as well as aiding recruitment. Others have formed display teams very recently, in particular countries such as China and Singapore where they have burgeoning aviation industries and it's exciting for the air show crowds to see new teams such as the Saudi Hawks, Al Fursan from the UAE and Thailand's Blue Phoenix.

At present there are a handful which are spoken about in the same breath as the Red Arrows, teams that have built a history from precision flying and spectacular performances and thrill crowds whenever they appear.

PATROUILLE DE FRANCE

The Patrouille de France is the oldest team in the world, being formed originally in 1931 at a flying school and flying Morane Saulnier MS-230 primary trainers. After the war they reformed and for most of their existence have flown French-built aircraft including the Dassault Ouragon, Mystere and the current aircraft since 1980, the Alpha Jet. This was built under a joint venture between Dassault and Breguet in France and Dornier in Germany.

The team gained its name in 1953 from an over excited air show commentator so that is now considered to be the formation date, the team celebrating its 60th anniversary in 2013.

The team is based at Salon de Provence

ABOVE At the 60th anniversary of the Patrouille de France in 2013 the leaders of the participating display teams fly for the cameras. (From foreground) Patrouille Suisse, Frecce Tricolori, Red Arrows, Patrouille de France, Patrulla Aguila, Team Iskra (Poland)

THE RED ARROWS HAVE COMPETITION!

and flies the unusual number of eight aircraft with one spare aircraft and pilot.

The last ten years have seen a number of firsts for the team. In 2007 they toured the Middle East for the first time. Two years later they not only took on a huge tour covering Brazil, Russia, South America and the Caribbean but also Virginie Guyot became the first woman to lead a national display team.

The Patrouille is all about skill and precision aerobatics with close formations flown beautifully.

US NAVY BLUE ANGELS

There are two national armed forces jet teams in the United States and the Blue Angels were formed just seven years before the Thunderbirds. They started in 1946 as the Navy Flight Exhibition Team flying the F6F Hellcat rapidly changing to the Bearcat, Panther, Cougar and Tiger before they took on the mighty Phantom in 1969. In fact they flew whatever was the front line aircraft of the US Navy at the time.

After 12 years on the Skyhawk the team converted to the F/A-18 Hornet, an aircraft which they have flown for more than thirty years. The team also uses a support aircraft which is part of their show. Their C-130 Hercules 'Fat Albert' is painted in the same colours as the Hornets, blue and yellow, and used to start the show with a spectacular jet assisted take off, or JATO, but the lack of rockets has left Fat Albert as the support aircraft carrying ground crew and spares to air shows.

The role of the Blue Angels is recruitment and the representation of US Navy and US Marine Corps aviation to the public. However budget cuts in recent years have meant that they fly less than before and even had to cancel the whole 2013 season.

Safety has sometimes been an issue for the team as they have lost twenty-six pilots during their performances and practices. That's about a 10% fatality rate, much higher than other teams. In 2011 the team was grounded and had to train intensively before they were allowed to fly in public again because they had performed a manoeuvre below safety limits. Shows were cancelled and the commanding officer stepped down.

However watching the Blue Angels is still an awe-inspiring sight and they represent the US armed forces with great style and precision.

FAR LEFT The oldest display team in the World, the Patrouille de France flying their Dassault / Dornier Alpha Jets, the fiercest competitor to the BAe Systems Hawk in the export market

THE RED ARROWS HAVE COMPETITION!

THE RED ARROWS HAVE COMPETITION!

IMAGE The US Navy's Blue Angels display team show how close they get in formation

USAF THUNDERBIRDS

The Thunderbirds were formed in 1953 just six years after the founding of the US Air Force. Similar to the Blue Angels they have always flown front line fighter aircraft rather than trainers. In the first few years they converted regularly, fly-ing Thunderjets, Thunderstreaks, Super Sabres and even Thunderchiefs for a few weeks. The Phantoms they received in 1969 would have stayed if it hadn't been for the worldwide oil crisis which forced them to change to the less thirsty T-38A Talon trainer. However in 1982 the Thunderbirds received their first

THE RED ARROWS HAVE COMPETITION!

F-16, an aircraft they have now flown for more than 30 years.

The Thunderbirds is a team of 12 officers and 120 enlisted men. There are eight pilots to fly the six aircraft, six team members and two reserves. The other four provide administrative, medical and PR support.

The team is known in the air force as America's Ambassadors in Blue. Everywhere they go they are representing the USAF. The whole display starts with choreographed movements and salutes and ends with all the pilots shaking hands with the support team. It's a well drilled presentation. In between

ABOVE The USAF Thunderbirds begin a line abreast loop during their display

THE RED ARROWS HAVE COMPETITION!

is a display of precision and panache as the white aircraft are flown in ultra close formations through a series of loops and rolls that show off the F-16 at its best.

The Thunderbirds seldom stray from the United States. It's seven years since they displayed in Europe and even their Far East tour in 2009 included displays at American bases such as Hawaii and Guam. But then they are paid for by the US taxpayers so it's the US public that should see them most.

THE SNOWBIRDS

While on the North American continent there is one more national display team definitely worth including. While the Snowbirds are Canada's national display team they are actually a single squadron. 431 Squadron RCAF is based at Moose Jaw in Saskatchewan.

The squadron's story dates back to the Second World War when it was formed as part of the RCAF contribution to Bomber Command of the Royal Air Force in 1942. Based in Yorkshire with many other Canadian squadrons 431 flew Wellingtons, Halifaxes and finally Lancasters. The squadron was disbanded after the war but reformed on Sabres in 1954. They were also responsible for displaying the abilities of the RCAF to the Canadian public. However they were soon disbanded again.

In 1969 at Moose Jaw the commander of Number 2 Canadian Forces Flying Training School saw formation flying as a way of enhancing training as well as providing flypasts at local events. To these informal flypasts they added a white Canadair CT-114 Tutor. By 1970 there were four, and in 1971 seven. The formations became bolder and manoeuvres were added to the displays. Eventually they adopted an official name in June 1971, one that came from a competition in a local school. The team was officially adopted by the RCAF in 1975 and in 1978 they were made into a proper squadron, 431 Air Demonstration Squadron.

The CT-114 Tutors are old now so although a total of only 24 people travel to displays there is a large team of fitters and engineers back at base constantly striving to keep the team in the air. On the continent they have flown everywhere from The Arctic, where they displayed at midnight on one occasion,

to Mexico. They fly nine white aircraft which look spectacular over the prairies and icy wastes of Canada as well as in the bright blue clear skies. The team represent teamwork, skill and professionalism. They also represent Canada extremely well.

PATRULLA AGUILA

The Patrulla Aguila, or Eagle Patrol in English, is the Spanish Air Force demonstration team, based at San Javier Air Base near La Manga on the east coast of Spain. The team fly Casa C-101 Aviojets, Spanish-built jet trainers which have been in service since 1980.

The team was formed in 1985 and have always flown the same aircraft. They have twelve aircraft but only fly seven in the team. For the first few years the aircraft used the same silver and orange colour scheme of all the other Spanish Air Force trainers. However, in time for the opening ceremony of the Barcelona Olympics in 1992 they

ABOVE The Spanish Air Force team, the Patrulla Aguila, parked behind the Red Arrows at Fairford for the 2006 RIAT

FAR LEFT Patrulla Aguila over El mar Menor with the Mediterranean in the background

ABOVE The Italian Air Force team, the Frecce Tricolori, showing why they are one of the most exciting display teams in the world

adopted a new scheme adding the yellow from the Spanish flag to the scheme.

To see the Patrulla Aguila display is a treat. Very precise they include some daredevil inverted formations in their routine, pouring yellow and red smoke in the colours of the national flag. Their displays are well choreographed and there is always something happening in front of the crowds.

FRECCE TRICOLORI

Italy is all flamboyance and colour and the Italian national display team, the Frecce Tricolori, is no different with bright blue and white aircraft, immaculately dressed pilots and crew, and red, white and green smoke pouring from the exhausts of their Aermacchi MB339 aircraft.

Formation flying has a long history in the Italian Air Force. Indeed the famous showstopper at Duxford's Flying Legends Air Show, the Balbo, is named after Italo Balbo the aviator who built up the Italian Air Force in the 1920s and pioneered the use of large formations over long distances by leading two formations of seaplanes on transatlantic flights in the early 1930s.

The Frecce was formed in 1961. In the same way the Red Arrows were created to avoid front line squadrons spending time on display flying the Italian Air Force stopped their unofficial teams from displaying and instead created the national team.

Initially they flew F-86 Sabres and then Fiat G-91s but converted to the Aermacchi MB339 in 1982 and have flown it ever since. The big blot on the Frecce's history was the mid-air collision at the Ramstein Air Show in Germany in 1988 that turned out to be the final air show ever flown in that country. The collision between three of their aircraft caused the death of all three pilots and 67 spectators.

They fly ten aircraft, that's more than any other team in the world. They have a solo and a nine ship formation. Strangely the commander of the team does not fly in it but has to have flown as a team member in the past. He is the charming, smiling public face of the team while the others get on and fly the formations.

The Frecce are very good at formations. They have a dynamic quality together with smooth transitions from one manoeuvre to the next that makes for constant action in the air. They wow the fans wherever they go and are experts at pleasing the crowd.

JUST A FEW

These are just six of the many teams that display all over the world. There are a number of things they all have in common.

They all only recruit the very best pilots who have many hours experience. That goes as well for the ground crews who keep the aircraft flying, sometimes for more than 100 displays in a year.

All teams have various display options depending on weather and make sure that even the flat show on a cloudy day is still spectacular viewing.

And most of all they are all fanatical about safety. Previous air show accidents have put safe displays in the spotlight. The detailed preparation and training is all designed to make sure that the right aircraft arrive at the right place exactly on time and perform a safe air show.

Display flying can be dangerous and it is good that only the best are asked to do it. Watching display flying is also great fun and hugely entertaining.

Chapter 10

Past, Present and Future

RIGHT The Red Arrows and French Patrouille de France in formation over Paris marking the 80th anniversary of President de Gaulle's speech on 18 June 1940. The flypast was repeated in London (Crown Copyright 2020)

In the last few years the Red Arrows have continued to perform to huge audiences. Their 2017 season consisted of 70 displays including a tour to eleven countries in just five weeks in the late summer. In support of the 'GREAT Britain' international marketing campaign they displayed at the Cannes Yachting Festival in the south of France, Athens Flying Week, flew over the great archaeological site of Petra in Jordan, followed by displays in Saudi Arabia, Kuwait, Doha, Muscat and Karachi with a tour-ending performance in Bahrain. At the end of that season Squadron Leader Martin Pert took over from David Montenegro as Red 1 and team leader. His three year tenure would be one of the most challenging to fall perhaps to any leader.

The 2018 season started with a tragedy when engineer Cpl. Jonathan Bayliss, flying in the back of David Stark's Hawk, was killed when the aircraft crashed soon after leaving RAF Valley on Anglesey on 20 March. Flt Lt David Stark ejected and suffered non-life threatening injuries but did not rejoin the team.

Later that same year perhaps the most important occasion for the team was as the centrepiece of the flypast over Buckingham Palace to celebrate the Centenary of the Royal Air Force, originally formed on 1 April 1918. 100 days after the Centenary itself, 10 July, the Red Arrows provided the stirring finale of a flypast of 100 aircraft.

RENEWING THE SPECIAL RELATIONSHIP

2019 was to be a huge year for the team. Disappointing their legion of fans up and down the UK, the Red Arrows cut short their usual UK season and took on an eleven week tour of North America for the first time since 2008. Leaving on 5 August they flew via Lossiemouth in Scotland, Keflavik in Iceland, Narsarsuaq in Greenland,

FAR LEFT The Red Arrows fly over the Queen Victoria Memorial in front of Buckingham Palace during the flypast for the Centenary of the Royal Air Force celebrations 10 July 2018 (Crown Copyright 2018)

LEFT The Red Arrows complete the flypast for the Centenary of the Royal Air Force celebrations 10 July 2018 (Crown Copyright 2018)

LEFT The Red Arrows over Petra in Jordan during Eastern Hawk (Crown Copyright 2017)

PAST, PRESENT AND FUTURE

BELOW The Red Arrows fly down the Hudson River with the backdrop of the Manhattan skyline in formation with two F-35 Lightning IIs and two F-22 Raptors (Crown Copyright 2019)

Goose Bay, Newfoundland and Halifax, Novascotia before undertaking flypasts, displays and ground events in 25 cities in Canada and the USA.

The tour, designed to enhance trade and investment between the UK, USA and Canada, included flights over Niagara Falls and the Golden Gate Bridge, displaying to an audience of more than three million who flocked to Huntington Beach, south of Los Angeles and major displays in Toronto, Vancouver, Chicago, St Louis, Dallas and San Francisco.

For many, however, the highlight was a flypast down the Hudson River and

round the Statue of Liberty in New York on 22 August. They flew in formation with the USAF official team of F-16s, the Thunderbirds, as well as two F-35 Lightning Its and two F-22 Raptors. Thousands packed the banks of the river to see this unique sight. After almost 22,000 miles in 74 days the team, together with it's support, arrived back at Scampton on 18 October.

ABOVE The Red Arrows over the Golden Gate Bridge in San Francisco during Western Hawk (Crown Copyright 2019)

THE YEAR IT ALL WENT WRONG

2020 should have been the swansong for Martin Pert with another packed season in the planning. However the arrival of the Covid-19 Coronavirus completely put paid to most of the plans. There was no Exercise Springhawk in Greece and their PDA, the Public Display Authority, was not granted until July in the vain hope that there would be an end of season after all.

There was no flying between 23 March and 12 April and then only single sorties were allowed purely to comply with regulations for safe flying proficiency. RAF Scampton was on lockdown and safe distancing was the order of the day.

Apart from some flypasts which did not need authorisation, the diary was empty. Three flypasts celebrated three important events. First was the 75th anniversary of VE Day in May, Next the 80th anniversary of President Charles de Gaulle's speech to the French people on 18 June 1940, which is considered as having spurred on the beginnings of the French Resistance. Finally, it was Armed Forces Day on 27 June. And that was it. Apart from the sterling efforts of the Shuttleworth Collection team at Old Warden to create Covid-safe shows there was no air show season.

Squadron Leader Martin Pert's last flight as Red 1 was on 9 October, purely a practice display, and perhaps not the correct send off for the leader of the team in the busiest, most challenging era of the team's history.

THE FUTURE

Since the dawn of the 21st Century, the RAF has changed considerably. The venerable old VC10 and Lockheed Tristar tankers have gone and the Airbus A330 Voyager replacement now serves with 10 and 101 Squadrons based at RAF Brize Norton. The Airbus A-400M Atlas strategic transport still suffers from technical issues but is planned to replace the C-130 Hercules fleet by 2023. The Jaguar, Harrier and Tornado have been retired and replaced by the Typhoon with the exciting Lockheed Martin F-35 Lightning II short take-off and vertical landing combat aircraft coming on stream. The RAF's OCU, 207, and first front line squadron, 617, are up and running while 809 Naval Air Squadron will give the Royal Navy a fixed wing capability for the first time since the Sea Harrier force was disbanded. In a period of joint operations, both RAF and Fleet Air Arm squadrons will operate from the Royal Navy's two new super carriers, Queen Elizabeth and Prince of Wales.

Future fast jet pilots continue to train on the Hawk with the introduction of the T.Mk.2 and that will continue at least until the 2030s. The T.2 features the digital cockpit which future pilots will use in their front line aircraft. That makes the Hawk compatible with the Typhoon and the Lightning II.

One major change for the Red Arrows will be their home. On 19 May 2020 it was announced that RAF Scampton is due to close and the Reds will move to their new base at RAF Waddington, one of the busiest RAF bases of all.

Waddington is the RAF's main base for the country's ISTAR capability. That's Intelligence, Surveillance, Target Acquisition and Reconnaissance. Many of the RAF's largest aircraft are based there. 8 Squadron operate the Boeing E-3D Sentry from Waddington as do 51 Squadron's Boeing RC-135W 'Rivet Joint' fleet. 14 Squadron's Beechcraft Shadow R1 base their intelligence gathering operations at Waddington as well as the ever increasing UAV force of 13 and 39 Squadrons. The Red Arrows will be obliged to fit into this very busy airfield. Luckily they will still be able to use Scampton's air space for their practices.

The Red Arrows, however, are always under threat. The team continue to fly Hawk T1s, some of the longest-serving aircraft in the RAF's fleet. but what they fly after that, or even whether the team will continue to exist, is dependent on many factors. BAE Systems, long-term sponsors of the team, are soon to cease production of the Hawk altogether so there is much less reason for them to commit to any financial backing. BAE is one of the many sponsors and supporters which include other aviation-related companies such as Rolls-Royce and Breitling.

It has been suggested that they could reform flying propellor-driven aircraft. At the other extreme they could fly the Typhoon or Lightning II, front line aircraft similar to the Thunderbirds and Blue Angels. After all, the future pilots vying for coveted places in the team each year are increasingly likely to come from Typhoon and Lightning II squadrons rather than any other aircraft.

At the heart of the argument is can the country afford to spend more than £10,000,000 every year on running a display team? Critics argue that it is difficult to defend redundancies and spending cuts on the front line if a display team is allowed to continue. However supporters say that the money is very little and that the benefits the team brings far outweigh the cost. That other great British aviation icon, Concorde, has disappeared from our skies. It would be a terrible day if the Red Arrows were to go as well.

Until that decision is made the Red Arrows will continue to fly spectacular air displays. They will represent the RAF and the country with the precision and skill that has marked their first 50 years of existence and still be the great entertainers.

Design & Artwork: ALEX YOUNG

Published by: G2 ENTERTAINMENT LIMITED

Publishers: JULES GAMMOND & EDWARD ADAMS

Written by: COLIN HIGGS